Fish Bones

GILLIAN SZE

Fish Bones

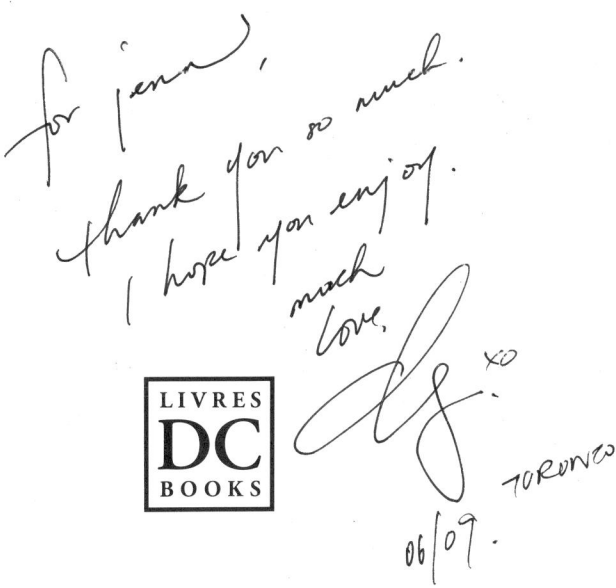

Cover art by Josée Bisaillon.
Author photograph by Eleftheria Spachis.
Book designed and typeset by Primeau Barey, Montreal.
Edited by Jason Camlot for the Punchy Writers Series.

Copyright © Gillian Sze, 2009.
Legal Deposit, Bibliothèque et Archives nationales du Québec
and the National Library of Canada, 1st trimester, 2009.

Library and Archives Canada Cataloguing in Publication
Sze, Gillian, 1985-
Fish bones / Gillian Sze.
(Punchy poetry)
Poems.
ISBN 978-1-897190-46-3 (pbk.)
ISBN 978-1-897190-49-4 (bound)
I. Title. II. Series: Punchy poetry.
PS8637.Z425F58 2009 C811'.6 C2009-901783-0

This is a work of art. Names, characters, places, and events are either products
of the author's imagination or are employed fictitiously. Any resemblance to actual
events or locales or persons, living or dead, is entirely coincidental.

No part of this publication may be reproduced or stored in a retrieval system
or transmitted in any form or by any means, electronic, mechanical, recording,
or otherwise, without written permission of the publisher, DC Books.

In the case of photocopying or other reprographic copying, a license must be
obtained from Access Copyright, Canadian Copyright Licensing Agency,
1 Yonge Street, Suite 800, Toronto, Ontario M5E 1E5 <info@accesscopyright.ca>

For our publishing activities, DC Books gratefully acknowledges the financial
support of the Canada Council for the Arts, of SODEC, and of the Government
of Canada through the Book Publishing Industry Development Program (BPIDP).

Canada Council   Conseil des Arts
for the Arts   du Canada

Société
de développement
des entreprises
culturelles

Québec

Printed and bound in Canada by Groupe Transcontinental. Interior pages
printed on 100 per cent recycled and FSC certified Enviro Print white paper.
Distributed by LitDistCo.

DC Books
PO Box 666, Station Saint-Laurent
Montreal, Quebec H4L 4V9
www.dcbooks.ca

for my family & friends

for you, listening

Contents

1	Cantaloupe
2	On Fleeing the Satyrs
3	The Last Time I Saw You
6	Beauty of an Eastern Dancer
7	Even the Maid Never Came
10	At the Picnic Barbecue
11	I'll Make the Drinks Tonight
15	The Kiss
16	Tending Ice Gardens
18	Remembering Lot's Wife
21	Forget-Me-Not
23	The Shepherd's Wife's Song
25	She Has a Lovely Face
28	fragmented
29	How To Be Dead
31	The Jailer's Daughter
32	To John Lyman and the Portrait of His Father
35	Coffee Talk
36	Our Heads: A Study
37	The Shepherdess's Lament
40	17th Floor
41	The Shaman's Dance
44	I Told Them that I Got to Keep the House
45	Child's Play
46	Animal Tracks
48	I Still Think So
49	Bird Watching

51 Alone on the Other Side of the World
52 Unaccompanied
56 The Rumoured Jar
57 Playing Fish Bones
60 Lunacy
61 The Changes Between

For the listener, who listens in the snow,
And, nothing himself, beholds
Nothing that is not there and the nothing that is.

Wallace Stevens

A fisherman's song is deep in the river.

Wang Wei

Cantaloupe

If you were here,
I would show you the cantaloupe
that my grandmother never meant to grow.

It just showed up by the rose bushes
like a mistake, some bastard child
that sprouted from an insatiable seed
thrown in with the compost.

It took root,
and the cantaloupe is no larger than a baseball,
the runt of the entire world's litter of fruit.

I would give it to you,
pass it into your hands, the way I do
with everything else. My feeble, crusted offerings:
striving for sweetness.

On Fleeing the Satyrs

Your legs need to pump so fast
your feet barely touch ground,
and ribbons will come undone
and your skirt will ignite.

You will lose feeling of everything
but for the hot blood in your legs,
the wind skimming the backs of your hands,
lacing through fingers.

Ignore the flowers
and their bodies *contrapposto,*
heads twisted on their necks.
Singed petals cool as they drop.

This is a race, don't look back.
To satyrs, you are a smudge of colour
spreading thin beneath
wavering clothes.

Run. Ignore their arms raised
in premature triumph.
Don't hesitate
for your outstripped shadow.

The Last Time I Saw You

I

When we were close enough
to confuse ourselves,
I mistook your nether region for hands.

II

Someone once wrote,
The earth moved.

Embracing you,
we rocked a boat
and the waves rushed upwards
past our heads,
reached the sky,
turned our hair into water.

And that clear heat—
even seaweed melted away
and found solace
at the edges of our bodies.

III

I wondered,
Can we make it as innocent as we'd like,
and suddenly we were naked,
pulled together by a trick law,
our bodies abiding by this new set of rules:

my legs forgot their joints,
you became four-fingered, three-toed,
and your hand matched the colour of your eyes,
matched the colour of mine,
our noses,
the shape of our skulls–
all sister copies,
even our lips pointed in the same direction.

Now tell me where I've put my foot,
and why the tide has become so high.

IV

The edge of your face,
a sliver of a silver dish.

The mole on the left side of your loins,
a baffling landmark.

V

Tears,
miraculous,
perfect in their fallen arrangement.

Autumn-coloured,
my tears bore the same shade as me,
and for a second,
I knew I was losing my border,
(my strokes once bold, unhesitant)
and you were made of pencil smudges–
unformed and consuming–
a proper place to deny distinction.

VI

How calm it looked behind you,
stormless and temperate.

How foolish of me
to try to define a horizon.

Beauty of an Eastern Dancer

The man I'm with likes to bite my hands,
leaves little red dashes on my knuckles
and along the bones of my fingers.

He pinches my breasts,
says they're so soft he only does it
to see if they're real.

>Afterwards, he asks me if it hurts,
>if it makes me suffer.

He's dressed me in gold,
twined lilies of the valley in my headpiece,
knotted tiny cymbals to my fingertips.

At night,
he unties the red strings from my thumbs.
He tries to unravel me.

But in the mirror
my dark eyebrows arch
like two halves of a bird,

and my hair
can hold a single, thick braid
on its own.

Even the Maid Never Came

I

Somehow,
it has become a favourite memory,
the white sheets assaulted by my skin,
by the inside of my body
as I wept.

The pillow unpressed,
the ashtray empty,
I put the plastic door hanger outside,
crossed off *Privacy Please*
and wrote:
Maid, please come.
Strip this bed.
The company could be nice.
I would even help you.
We can make small talk.

I waited three days,
stared at the blue floral trimming,
its monotony.
Its monotony was trying to tell me something
I didn't know,
or maybe something I did,
but didn't want to.

II

When I hung up on you,
the sun at the foot of the bed
flipped the shadows backwards
behind me.

The carvings of the night table
made ghosts
shaped like medicine bottles
against the walls.
The dark can be mocking
in conversation.

Cradling the phone,
I pressed my face against
the rotary dial.

The glare
made two bright spots
on the uneven wallpaper.
I let the spy stay in my wall.

III

A twin bed,
I would've made space for you.

I would've given you my pillow.
I would've smoked with you.

In this bible
we would've written over God's name
with our own,
we would've ordered everything on the drink menu,
cavorted in a pile of bottles, corks
and toothpick umbrellas.

And we could've cut the cord to this red phone,
climbed the roof,
pitched it,
and when I heard the last shard settle,

I would've forgiven you.

At the Picnic Barbecue

You were mistreating words again,
courting my eyes
with moonstruck descriptions,
calling them *puce,*
silver spoons,
sun-streaked glass.

In the crowd,
your voice became muted,
receded into the backdrop,
so I heard just the occasional thwack
like the wash,
tumbling in the dryer.

I overheard you say,
She looks sad—
it's in her face.

The truth is,
I looked up
when they called out, *Ready!*
and I finished my third glass of sangria,
because I was hungry,
and it was time to eat.

I'll Make the Drinks Tonight

I

My current lover–
> she is nothing like you.

II

Your house:
an old slanted duplex in Little Italy,
with doors held open by hooks.
We watched dropped olives roll
to the back of the kitchen,
and morning greeted me with
a fall into the facing wall,
a slumber-drunk tip,
the sound of my banging shoulder.

Cat hairs swept to corners,
above a basement smelling of cat shit and mould.
This was where your ex-husband left you,
dressed in your cotton black dress
and tan boots,
a cocktail in one hand,
unsuspecting.

III

Your bed:
princess-style
and three feet off the ground,

a duvet
feather-flush and packed with air,
pillows pillows pillows.

A white lagoon
where we dipped,
your fallen frame,
all bones and hips and elbows,
the perfect placement of your knees between mine.

We were born together a thousand times
when the music from your antique gramophone
crackled over our naked limbs.

IV

My current lover is simple
with an unremarkable history
she has effortlessly set free.

She doesn't mix her alcohol,
doesn't eat anything off the floor.
She memorized what I wore
the first time she saw me.
She is Reason
in a pair of ironed jeans,

and she is *she,*
an impossibility
for her to take your place
as *you.*

V

One night the rain broke in
through a forgotten window.
A line of pills beside snuffed candles.
My paintings were framed
but still on your floor.

You said,
No one speaks Hazel.
Your name,
a language even you were only half-fluent in,
pink lips practicing the shapes of sounds.
Before you passed out
you told me,
Well, they do.
But only for a little while.
Then they forget the words.

That night
your disappointment chaperoned sleep and me,
keeping us at arm's distance.
Your quiet gulps marked the hours,
and I watched you toss
and then finally stand up,
languid and feline.

> I tell my lover this over dinner
> while the lady seated behind us

in her Brooklyn accent
argues with her husband about change.

And in the broken language of my name,
my lover tells me,
*Well, I am glad she had that bed.
I would cry if she didn't.*

VI

Through the crack in the bathroom door,
you stretched;
your eyes closed as your face
tipped up to the light.
Beauty thrown back,
you shrugged it off,
discarding it like underwear.

You were perched,
with your back to the mirror,
your weight in the heels of your hands
at the edge of the sink,
down the curve of your calf;
your pointed toes
were all that touched the floor.

And then I knew,
never again
would I know anything so purely
as the blunt end of your chin,
pointed to the ceiling.

The Kiss

mouths gulp, gorge in slick struggle,
breaths swallow full,

eyelashes strain to meet.

Tending Ice Gardens

Memory is monochrome,
white-hoofed,
playing film stills
on his bare erection.

Spotting me,
he is the opposite of blushing.
Earth becomes spongy,
a mire beneath his feet sprouting buds
like halves of cracked eggshells.

I suppose if I had to colour it,
I'd make this white, too:

Her short silver locks,
cheeks like coconut pulp,
the white tips of her nails
prodding past your undershirt,
the pale polka-dots on her skirt,
the stucco wall a stage set for your felony.

In the small lustre at the upper curve of your ear,
I spied clean white feet,
bare undersides,
alabaster sheets,
the milk in a dandelion,
the scar on your chin
the innocent flick of a light switch.

How I never thought
an iceberg could sprout inside me,
eight-ninths immersed inside my ribcage

and how wicked Memory plays the tip,
melting pasty-grins,
shell shock white,
so furious and suffocating.

Remembering Lot's Wife

I

From the hill,
I stared down at the
broken limbs
of the city.

It wilted,
a flower in a sun too strong,
what it was before,
smouldering
and already forgotten.

The sky was bleeding,
sizzling where it touched ground.
Outside the city,
the unscorched land was mirrored
to the dancing flames,
lit by sun
and bordered by shadows.

The birds drifted in ash clouds,
their silhouettes difficult to distinguish
whether they were flying
away or returning.

II

Our last night,
our hair,
a long tangle between us.
When we lay side by side
the quiet made me ill,
and I rolled on top of you,
your breasts supple,
shaping themselves against mine.

I whispered,
I am scared you will evaporate.

So I stayed there,
aligning our curves
(our breasts between our weight,
our hips, hugging only each other),
and pressed closer,

a sheathe
for where you once were.

III

I saw white streaks in the blaze.
I saw a man with arms outstretched
and face wet and sooty.
I saw a cow seared,
its bones left for crows.
I saw a couple hovering in a cave,
their packed trunk, the only thing left.
I saw the distance, blue and peaceful.
I saw the sun's face in the ground.

And then I saw you,
your hair loose,
the heel of each step
a dirty departure,
before you slowed,
the figures of your children
diminishing,

and then you turned.

I watched you crumble.
Your sweetness turned to salt,
your name dissolved on my tongue,
tasting like you dropped from my eyes.

Forget-Me-Not

His wife has returned
from her trip to Peru,
and he is flipping through photos
listening to her shuffle around the kitchen
her voice excited and practiced,
the sights already told
over and over again.

He is looking at stelae,
ceramic portraits,
panpipes,
and stops at the figurine
with a head like a half-set sun
baked flat,
eyebrows spreading ear to ear,
and arms made of two knobs.

He doesn't hear his wife
carry on about Machu Picchu,
or the helicopter rides,

he can only remember
being seventeen
standing on his front porch
with the girl,
her stomach flat and defiant,
blowing smoke between her words
saying, *Even if I stopped taking them,*

it'd come out dumb and limbless—
and watched her
grind the lit end against the railing.

Only now
does he discover
that the possibility to forget
is as brief as his reflection
on the window of a closing door.

The Shepherd's Wife's Song

You have gone again
to meet the moon,
its form orbed
and pouched with wait.

In this light,
the dog is mistaken
for a patch of grass,
the sheep's heads
aglow and saintly.

From this distance,
the mauve-blue hills
and silent hay bales
would seem irenic
in the fog,

but nearby
the washerwoman moans,
her love-cries
scattering dandelions,

and above,
the moon is a yellow concussion,
the sky in protest,
its colour turning peach,
pink,
the inside of your hands.

And you have gone again
to the end of the meadow
where the hills are darkest,

with my blue scarf
tucked in your sleeve,
your face dusky
like the underside of the moon.

She Has a Lovely Face

"And as the boat-head wound along
The willowy hills and fields among,
They heard her singing her last song,
The Lady of Shalott."
Alfred Tennyson

I. The Tower

The afternoon was cutting
like ripe citrus.

In the heat,
I thought you romantic,
that someone who still scythed
must also keep chickens.

Up the road,
your hair shone dark as blackcurrants.
I confused the barley you shook out
for strips of sun.

Behind the heap of sheaves,
we kneeled and you flipped the card:
a tower burned by lightning,
two figures falling to the ground.

Change, you said. *Revelation.*
You told me what I already knew;

our naked fever
still cooling amidst the reaping.

Is love not the change
from which our days are reconditioned?
In my tapestry,
I weave a blazing tower.
I am the figure, white-clad and falling.

You stand at the bottom,
head back,
face traced by flames,
a simple spectator.

II. Seven of Cups

I wove by day,
breaking to lift the hair
off the back of my neck,
to make space for wishful thoughts.

Did you doubt me
when I said we were dreamers–
who else but those too-edged with hope,
sing conversations by moonlight?

You heard me in the rye,
I heard you at the loom.
In the cups, I repeated your face
in stitches seven times.

And when that sun-pierced shadow
passed so close, trilling a song,
I rose to search for you
in the crowded bend.

No one blamed Orpheus
for looking back, except Orpheus.

III. The Chariot

You told me of the paintings,
the variations of the same scene,
how someone finally told you the secret
—how to find me:

Just look for the rower.

Before lining myself in the boat,
I ripped my weaving from the loom,
the unfinished chariot and rider,
two yoked sphinxes with my face.

From my window I dropped it,
and its images stretched in the air,
flitted away.

You never said if you saw it,
fraying and catching light,
if you even paused in those long fields,
to wonder what it was.

fragmented

This city has me by the ankles.
It has dragged me through the streets
in a heated mad dash.

I have found bitefuls of me on the curb,
scraps of me in the gutter.
That is my hair blown across
the glass angles of downtown.
A bird has made a nest with the strands
so I now live in the trees,
curled beneath fledglings,
and I am part-statue,
part church-top.
My eyes, once copper domes,
have since turned green.
My hands are worn
by every woman
working at a corner store.
My mouth is on the morning metro man,
and everyone who tastes my thighs
has done it
at least once before.

This city has me by the ankles.
I'm pounded flat and pinned fast,
a pasted broadside on every lamppost.

How To Be Dead

The morning after you died,
I almost got hit
crossing the street by my home;
so close
I thought maybe I was a ghost
walking unseen
down the street on garbage day,

past shapeless black, plastic masses,
broken table legs,
a denim covered mattress,
past a girl wearing big headphones, crying,
past the usual man on the corner
who didn't ask me for change
for the first time,

and I wished someone would meet my eyes,
offer me a flyer,
hold the door a moment longer,

because what would I have to do
to get noticed
if not light myself in flames
and sing a song off-key?

I suppose I'd find the good in it,
like the Egyptians
with their book of the dead,
and learn how to pass you again
to make it right.

All this was pathetic,
(to be alive and know it–

confirmed by an old lady
accepting my seat on the bus),
and the next day I woke up feeling gritty,
so I took my sheets to the balcony,
and thrashed out all the sand,
even if imaginary.

The Jailer's Daughter

She is everywhere,
this lady,
made of sticks
and thick black strokes.

In mid-air,
about to complete a cartwheel,

reclining backwards
on a chaise longue,

leaning over a raised knee
with her backside whipped out,

pin-up posed,
kneeling devoutly at the foot of the bed,

leaping, one leg so far back it touches her head,

singing, *I dreamed I was a jailer's daughter*
in capital letters,

and isn't her face so delightful,
how could anybody not notice her?

To John Lyman and the Portrait of His Father

I

I meant to write something that said,
Yes, I know what you mean.

Your father sitting there, dark and broad,
like the old rock at the riverfront by my house.
The deliberate crossing of his legs,
his spectacles balanced on a hard bridge,
a left elbow digging into the cushioned arm.

He's been keeping a shadow in his shirt pocket.

Your painting:
I think, chiselled stone.
I think, a firm *no.*
I think of my father's straight gaze
out the living room window,
cutting off the breath of the boy
talking with me at the end of the driveway.

The metal rim of eyeglasses.
The worn edges of our kitchen chairs.

Your father sat there reading when you painted him.
My father stopped when he was only two pages in.

II

Did they both sigh, I wonder,
when they found out who their children really were?

III

A river is cold in the prairies.
The water moves north.
The current is crimson,
strong, a dictator
moving along lost mittens, shoes,
stirring stories of how the river got so red,
collecting the spit of kids leaning over the bridge railing.

A river works in tradition.

I left carrying my father's prediction:
me, grown up and malnourished.
Spending days on the street corner,
ignored by passers
and begging to sketch their portraits.

IV

I meant to write something that said,
Yes, I know. Someone had blundered and it wasn't me.

V

Yesterday I learned about my grandfather.
How he crossed a bay into Malaysia to marry again,
abandoning his first family in China as a false start.

And my own dad, fourteen,
going over to search for a missing person.

This is where a sigh is born:
on the shores of a strange country
and nurtured in water;
practiced as an immigrant,
natural as a middle-aged man
and making up most of what I remember.

VI

The river is loud. It is a long moan.
This isn't what I meant to write.
The river lifted that and deposited its dregs elsewhere.

Somewhere back there a man birthed an unspeakable name.
Somewhere a man grows old and resembles a boulder from
 childhood.
Somewhere I hear of a river being blamed for draining a lake.

Now the current has moved me down the river line.
The rock by my home is gone from sight.

Coffee Talk

We left your mother's,
cut through the schoolyard
where boys in black hoodies congregated,
looking innocent,
staring at their feet in the snow.

Last night's fight echoed
in the morning bareness:
>the cold stone table,
>two bicycles abandoned against the fence,
>a black garbage bag whipped by the wind,
>the road stencilled with tire tracks,
>a white target spray-painted on the concrete wall.

In the middle of the street I peeked over at you,
my sight fitting only the brim of your blue wool cap,
my hands in little-kid gloves cupping my half-empty coffee.
My only dialogue–a request for sugar and cream–
collected in a Styrofoam cup.

Reaching the other curb,
I offered you a sip,
my coffee, an olive branch–
only learning then
how words can run out
so early in the morning.

Our Heads: A Study

The shape of our crowns,
a figure eight,
a peach split open.

You:
a drop of rain concussed on concrete.

Me:
glancing off when you landed,
fallen alongside,
fallen lucky,
just missing the sidewalk crack.

And today,
yesterday's geometry
is the cast of two eggs–
their absence
barely touching.

The Shepherdess's Lament

for Judith

I

Sprawled on this rock,
the sun is burning my hair and heating my back
like a heavy hand commanding sleep.

My sheep have swarmed and settled by my feet
and when I open my eyes again
I think that I have mistakenly climbed
to the top of a mountain.

The bright afternoon sweeps through the valley.
It is just me, my flock,
and the wind's empty song.

II

The old shepherd said,
Here, you take the flute.
I will sing you the song of withered Daphnis.

I flung away the pipes,
pulled him by his two drooping earlobes
and said,
If you stay a little longer,
then I will sing you the saddest songs
that I've hummed quietly only to myself.

III

It was too easy to call her lavender,
rose water,
laurel.

She was the taste of goat milk,
subtle as a bite of cantaloupe.

When she asked me to be more exact,
I said I couldn't find the words.

Give me another word for *tree,*
you'll see that you can't find one.

IV

In my sleep,
she lets me re-tell the same stories to her:

the ordinary memories of lying on our backs
in conversation with the moon,

how we were happiest in the company of a single dog,
a sheep, the call of a wood-pigeon.

She would reach up to pin down the stars,
fix them to the dark with her finger.

I awaken with my hands outstretched,
scraping nothing but sky.

V

I still reach for her,
when the vale winds drive the dandelions into shock,
when leaves float slowly down like the best sort of rain.

But Death has served me from a wooden spoon,
and the quick slip of a lemon seed from between my lips
has left my mouth hollow and sour.

I've worn the months heavy around my neck.
I've found nothing pleasing in a handful of glow worms.

17th Floor

Through the window the city is muted.
Smoke billows in slow motion.

Silence tempers the world listless,
makes it easier to bear.

Even that plane is hardly moving
through the quiet sky.

The birds have lost their voices
in the cold.

The Shaman's Dance

I

From my kitchen window, I see
someone's left a stroller in the alleyway,
a man pull flattened cardboard boxes out of a dumpster,
the trees' bareness open to the sky's scalp.

Winter skims the streets,
hides beneath stoops and by fire escapes,
whips the leaves off the pavement.
It cools the mug between my hands.

Now the world is changing–
when void-eyed strangers search,
turn to God,
to their morning black coffee,
to the constancy of missing socks.

II

Tonight I came home to a blinking light.
Your recorded voice flooded the room,
telling me that you've left.

You were calling from a train heading west to Toronto,
and it will be dark when you pass the Great Lake,
the sun setting earlier now, at four o'clock.

That is the little joy I can find,
the only good reason to have been left behind.

III

Columbia is the world's kidnapping capital.
As I get older, I come closer to passing it,
a part of me snatched by men,
myself compromised:

> standing at the end of a soccer field,
> in an elevator going down,
> at my desk,
> while smoking my last cigarette on the balcony,
> when I am within earshot of them as they put on
> their shoes,
> or pay the tab
> or not pay at all.

I am sampled,
a bit of me stuffed in the shaman's hollow bone
and capped with bark
then pocketed,
fastened to their house key,
pressed between pages of a borrowed book.

IV

In the middle of the night,
I leave my tiny apartment with my jacket open
flapping back.

The meagre leaves above me glow red in streetlight,
ahead of me is a woman with short hair,
arms linked with a man–

she is propped against him,
but they turn to each other in unison,
smile,
their eyebrows spring together in secret,

and she raises a hand to stroke his beard,
the motion regular
soothing
painful to watch.

I Told Them that I Got to Keep the House

The kids have moved out now,
I've repainted the bathroom,
bought a new bed,
equipped the kitchen with a blender,
reupholstered the love seat

but your clothes are still in the closet,

and every year
when the weather changes
and I put away the season's clothes,
I take the time
to pull out your best white shirt for one night,
iron and hang it for you on the back of the door
and pretend that by morning
I'll wake up to find it gone.

Child's Play

Recollections rippled,
awake by a heavy breath.

He is winding himself through
the bottom ends of reflections,
the fragments of objects overlapping.

In this broken pond
is his childhood:
the barn on that side,
the apple orchards on the other,
with her homemade dress, cherry red.
In the middle is hay, newly baled,
a piece of azure sky at the bottom
tells him the time of day.

That morning,
past the netted blueberry bushes,
and between the rows of corn,
the girl from the next house
down the road,
bent down
and pulled up her skirts.

He stared into the stream
before testing his fingers,
catching the trickle
in the cup of his hand,
the scent fierce and engulfing–

the moment ceased,
her skirt fell back down to her knees
and he felt the sun, hot on his head.

Animal Tracks

My sister has left her new condo,
found home in our parents' old cottage,
a small dwelling in the mountains
with not enough windows.

At the beginning
it was just a sweaty Tuesday night
when I watched her scribble a note to herself
to call the hospital
make an appointment
solve what the nurse meant
when she said,
There are atypical cells
in your test results.

Now I visit her for the first time
and she has on a ragged shawl
her roots are showing,
all making her look
inappropriate.

We hike out to our log
in the middle of the brush.
She has come to sound like our father
pointing out a small path crossing ours
telling me that it's an animal trail.
When I ask what animal,

she says, *We'd have to study its tracks,
take a look at its shit—*

isn't that how it goes for everything?

Her laugh is crippled
and I feel like I did that night
when she returned from the hospital
armed with two bottles of wine.
My courage suddenly laughable
like one child yelping to the other,
Make it go away, make it go away.
But I stayed quiet
even then
when she reached across the table
to refill her cup,
her hand trembling
between a candle flame
and a full glass of wine.

I Still Think So

I was nine
when I discovered
that I looked prettier
in photographs
when they were turned
upside down.

Bird Watching

At the back of the art gallery
where no one ventures,
a spotlight kindles the air,
lights up a pair of birds.

Here in this part of the room,
their presence is reticent
and I suddenly feel accountable,
a trespasser
where the sticker on the wall
(a hand crossed out)
implies more than forbidding touch.

☙

Love on a pedestal,
you said when we first saw the birds.
Your voice broke the unerring quiet,

broke the same way when months later,
you told me that you were sorry
to have fallen in love with another woman.

Sorry.

Like the same word
fit for a stranger to use
for getting in your way

could be as amending,
your misplaced love rendered fixable.

☙

The august curves of their necks
bear down on a chest amalgamated.
Thin staff-limbs join into one stump.
Where their beaks barely touch are they distinct:
an opening
fit for an arrowhead,
a forked heart.

Their tails match in blunted curves,
each wooden wing painfully split,
proof that Time cracks vertically,
the eroded wood's up-and-down splintering
like how a heart is broken:
down the center
and through one half of you.

Alone on the Other Side of the World

Tonight you feel farther than ever.
Distance is a hard man to blame,
like when one has a bad dream
about the real people around him.

My mind has started playing tricks.

I woke up diagonally in my bed,
my coordinates aligned with yours,
and when the cashier wished me a good day,
I thought he said, *You look lonely.*

All I want to tell you
is that I miss you.

You would think that I would know
how to use the words
properly.

This night is a scam and my shadow
has sleepwalked ahead of me;

the sound of somebody in the house
is just a moth
hitting against the inside of a lampshade.

Unaccompanied

I

August again

and the only letter in my mailbox
is a cautionary piece
about lead in my drinking water.

II

August brings bottles of wine
sipped in solitude,
and the familiar shape of your name
in unfamiliar places.

It brings dreams,
mundane, like us in a car
or talking on the phone.

In one dream,
you have a new tattoo
of a worm dangling in front of a fish.

You called this *waiting*.

And for the rest of that day,
all I could think of
was how easy you were to love
when you were folding a bed sheet,
your arms spread full-span.

III

Someone once said
when two people are in love
they create a third being

and that when it's over and done,
the third is left to wander.

IV

She is an offprint of me,
separate
yet close enough to cry for,
with the same face,
a shared expectation
we shadow on ourselves.

I wonder how we will break,
the end of our dance as we sever.
I wonder how we look from afar,
our melded shape
like the silhouette of coral,
a horse's head,
or the bottom half of a man's face.

I wonder what it is
that makes us put meaning
into objects and dates.

A bright, cloudless Sunday,

a bouquet of sunflowers,
a bed frame,
a broken shell.

The light is real,
hitting her back
smooth
in strains and spine.

She is my third:
haunting,
crying into the clean pillow beside me
and keeping me up at night.

V

I filter my water now—
twice before I drink it.

In the paper,
I read about a woman in New York
who dropped a spoon in her kitchen.

When she bent down,
her house exploded,
and amidst the debris of fate and luck,
she crawled out safely
from beneath her kitchen counter.

I should make use of this,
to let go of the spoon
and save myself in some small way,
but it is nearly the end of August,

and it is quiet
except for the heave of a passing truck,
and it is the sort of night
where I will try to sleep
with good intentions for myself,
starting in the morning.

The Rumoured Jar

"The jar was gray and bare."
Wallace Stevens

You placed the jar on my navel
then stepped back
and stood by my feet.

Your face warped sorely
through the old and bubbled glass:
a tumour on your chin,
a pit in your head,
but nothing too different.

Now the story's all wrong.
My body isn't yours to express,
not for you to map out
what did or didn't.

The wilderness did rise,
it sat upright
in graceful repose.
Smoothly, it upset nothing.

What is new
and what is ordered
is not in the jar,
but in how I've capped it
with an open mouth
and learned to swill the air.

Playing Fish Bones

I

The open mouth of the cup
is a flattened moon.

Tea is poured
and the cup returns
to being an ordinary teacup,
small and chaste,
its porcelain exterior decorated
with a woman snuggling a rabbit,
her hand up
in a gesture that declines a man
whose outstretched arm
offers a flower.

II

Talk is polishing the phone lines,
the same news worn down between relatives.

When I visit,
my mother's sister is dressed in thick wool,
her hair ink-black at sixty.
She is still pushing plums on me,
nectarines,
the watermelon she's already sliced into cubes.

A prickled impatience:

I am nine again, tied to a piano,
my fingers working the scales,
hours before my parents return from work.

My aunt's movements fluid,
I forget the muted exchanges:
… she only travels to find a doctor overseas…
… her bowels… an operation…

She leaves the kitchen
only to yell after her grandchildren to wear jackets,
the summer sun baking their backs as they pedal away
from where she leans against the doorframe.

III

A brown rim has set.
My tea slowly half-finished.

From her pocket,
my aunt reveals a bracelet.

She has collected the round bones of salmon,
plucked and saved from at least eight dinners.
She cleaned them,
picked marrow from the crevices with a toothpick,
dried them in the sun before another wash
then strung them together with red thread
and placed it here beside uneaten fruit.

IV

The tea is cold.
In silence I finish it off,
fake apathy.

The bracelet is a mouth forced open.
I fix my gaze on my cup,
tilting its hollow space towards me.
The same figures, same woman and man,
painted smaller to fit at the bottom,
suddenly look more amiable.
The span between refusal and acceptance
shrinks in an instant,
differs by only a fraction.

Lunacy

Behind the buildings,
the sky is like verdigris above the horizon.
The last year rusted through, I wake early.
Raise my green tea to the moon.
It looks down with a half-closed eye.

Lately, I've been more aware
of the moon's phases.
We are somewhere between a new moon
and the first quarter,
and I find myself at intersections
seeking a sliver of shaded relief
behind the blinds.

I am all middle-ground,
flanked by the urgency of language,
the tremor
and the salacity that swings above it.

A full moon will sprout in two weeks.
They say its effects usually last for four days.
People on the street will shift just as I pass,
this dementia will be a lighter bearing.

The Changes Between

(a crown of sonnets)

for E.D.O.

I feel your hands
where they've never been:
soft against the open land....
The length of the continent's body
is laid out between us. Lean over, gaze at it.
Anne Simpson

I. A Backwards Departure

Take-off is always the difficult part.
Angled back, feeling heavy,
knowing it is not just the weight of the sky,
but something inside, knocked out of place.

I already miss your face,
laughing green eyes set in a pallid moon.
This is being alone: sitting next to a stranger,
my home reduced to a window seat.

I am thinking about lights while trying to forget
how I can't remember my mother's eyes.
Lights: if there is one for every person in the world
thinking of you, bulbs would scatter a map.

Today there will be one single light moving steadily by,
so bright you could mistake it for the sun.

II. Re-familiarize

So bright you could mistake it for the sun,
the bus is still yellow and orange,
reminding me of when I was ten,
just learning to ask the driver for a transfer.

At the red light my mother asks about the flight.
I tell her that I slept through it, and when I woke up,
I saw the hard terrain, cut and grooved by little streams,
the strewn square patches of farm.

From up there,
bare land poked out from the snow
and for a moment I could squint,
pretend they were an archipelago, locked in a lake.

Look. The power lines, the telephone poles, I point out.
She tells me they've always been here.

III. This is Close to Home

She tells me they've always been here,
the rabbits in the garden;
their prints in the snow
lead somewhere behind my shed.

The trucks have always been here,
the church by the train tracks,
the mall's low wooden ceilings, its strung tinsel,
the stores' flat, plastic, rectangle signs.

At Zellers, I'm sure the middle-aged woman
with her blue eye shadow and frosted lips
has always been here, along with the Robin's Donuts lady,
tired brown face and missing her two front teeth.

Shoppers Drugmart still has the old logo;
its squatness, no space for excuses.

IV. After the Art Gallery, He Tells Me I Wasted His Time

Its squatness, no space for excuses,
my older brother's mind
is shaped to be analytical,
efficient, rigid.

His first encounter with the word "resonant"
was in physics class, a lecture on frequencies.
He asks me repeatedly, *Do you people ever dispute
whether something is more resonant or more echoing?*

He watches me jot down Rodin:
*True artists are almost the only men who do their work
    for pleasure.*
My brother is quiet in his laughter and whispers,
Sounds like a serial killer to me.

He wears an iron ring on his pinky now.
This returning feels imaginary.

V. Tell Me Where I Fit

This returning feels imaginary.
An Irishman born on a boat, you come from a line
   of mermaids.
My blood streams from somewhere with its own strangeness,
descendent of an emperor's lust.

My mother stashes her wine and vodka in paper bags
on the floor of her yarn and linen closet.
She eats eleven gin-soaked-raisins every morning
to treat her arthritis.

The cabinets are cramped with tea,
there are rabbits in my backyard, still an apple on the tree,
Hey—you across the street—you grew up nicely, come out and play,
the neighbour's brown trimming is peeling.

At night, do you recall the angles of my shoulders?
The ratio of my hips to yours?

VI. He is the Silent Type; He Silences Me

The ratio of my hips to yours
is a number approaching one.
Pry me away, put me back under his roof,
watch me diminish to something less.

My father is a young ghost, only four years old,
born just a few months before I left.
I can barely feel him when he walks by
but I still get cold when I hear the thud of his boot.

Older here, I appreciate the small things:
the foreign quiet when he and I are in a room,
my mother free to wash rice in the kitchen,
my kid brother, grown up now, knows not to hit girls.

Christmas goes by slowly like sipping oolong tea.
The new year passes through like a draft.

VII. I've Done This Once Before

The new year passes through like a draft
and I find myself packing for my flight,
my mother is cross-legged on the floor beside me,
stuffing roasted almonds in the gaps.

My father paces in the hallway,
he doesn't pause to look in.
This is the only way he knows how to remember:
a sidelong view through a doorway.

On board, I sit next to a boy whose hair curls over his ears.
When we speed up, I catch him crossing himself.
I'm Catholic, he shrugs, eyes on his lap.
You have one of those for me too?

He crosses himself again.
Take-off is always the difficult part.

Notes

The beginning epigraphs come from Wallace Stevens' poem, "The Snow Man," and Wang Wei's poem, "About Old Age."

"Remembering Lot's Wife" is based on the biblical story, "Sodom and Gomorrah."

The epigraph for "She has a Lovely Face" is from Alfred Tennyson's "Lady of Shalott."

"The Rumoured Jar" is inspired by Wallace Stevens' poem, "Anecdote of the Jar."

The epigraph for "The Changes Between" is from Anne Simpson's "Flying East." The quote in sonnet IV ("True artists are almost the only men ....") is from Auguste Rodin.

Acknowledgements

This book emerges from my engagement with artworks housed in Musée des Beaux-Arts de Montréal, Collection Musée d'art Contemporain de Montréal, Galerie d'art Yves LaRoche, Art Gallery of Ontario, The Power Plant, and The Winnipeg Art Gallery. I would like to express my gratitude to the artists (deceased, living, or anonymous) who provided me that first spark. I am honoured to partake in this "process of interchange" between art-objects, and I hope that these poems hold up as worthy responses to different conversations.

ಜಿ

Some poems from this collection have appeared or will appear in *Prairie Fire, Headlight Anthology 11, Asian Cha,* and the Asia and Pacific Writers' Website.

"fragmented" was featured as "The Parliamentary Poem of the Week" selection.

ಜಿ

My sincerest gratitude to my editor, Jason Camlot, for his insight, enthusiasm and good humour. My warmest thanks to Mary di Michele, David McGimpsey, John Steffler, André Furlani, Mikhail Iossel, Judith Herz, David Bergen and Andrew Shchudlo for their valued encouragement. To those who offered criticism regarding some of these poems (especially the Wednesday-night-workshop) thank you all. I am grateful to my friends for their love and confidence. I am especially indebted to Alison Strumberger for her sensitive and considered appraisal, and S. for reminding me that I belong right where I am.

Thanks to my family for their support. To my parents, Tina and Henry, for encouraging me to learn. To my brothers, Edmond and Edwin, for always providing a safe haven.

Gillian Sze was born and raised in Winnipeg, Manitoba. Her poetry has appeared in such venues as *CV2, Prairie Fire, pax americana* (US), *Crannóg* (Ireland), *Cha: An Asian Literary Journal* (Hong Kong), and as a featured "Parliamentary Poem of The Week" selection. She is also the author of two chapbooks, *This is the Colour I Love You Best* (2007) and *A Tender Invention* (2008). She has an M.A. in Creative Writing from Concordia and resides in Toronto.